KU-611-899

BUSTING BOREDOM
IN THE GREAT OUTDOORS

BY TYLER OMOTH

raintree

a Capstone company — publishers for children

Raintree is an imprint of Capstone Global Library Limited, a company incorporated in England and Wales having its registered office at 264 Banbury Road, Oxford, OX2 7DY – Registered company number: 6695582

www.raintree.co.uk
myorders@raintree.co.uk

Text © Capstone Global Library Limited 2017
The moral rights of the proprietor have been asserted.

All rights reserved. No part of this publication may be reproduced in any form or by any means (including photocopying or storing it in any medium by electronic means and whether or not transiently or incidentally to some other use of this publication) without the written permission of the copyright owner, except in accordance with the provisions of the Copyright, Designs and Patents Act 1988 or under the terms of a licence issued by the Copyright Licensing Agency, Saffron House, 6–10 Kirby Street, London EC1N 8TS (www.cla.co.uk). Applications for the copyright owner's written permission should be addressed to the publisher.

ISBN 978 1 4747 3690 9
21 20 19 18 17
10 9 8 7 6 5 4 3 2 1

British Library Cataloguing in Publication Data
A full catalogue record for this book is available from the British Library.

Every effort has been made to contact copyright holders of material reproduced in this book. Any omissions will be rectified in subsequent printings if notice is given to the publisher.

All the internet addresses (URLs) given in this book were valid at the time of going to press. However, due to the dynamic nature of the internet, some addresses may have changed, or sites may have changed or ceased to exist since publication. While the author and publisher regret any inconvenience this may cause readers, no responsibility for any such changes can be accepted by either the author or the publisher

Acknowledgements
Alesha Sullivan, editor; Kyle Grenz, designer; Morgan Walters, media researcher; Katy LaVigne, production specialist; Marcy Morin and Sarah Schuette, project producers

Photo Credits
Capstone Studio: Karon Dubke, 5, 7, 9, 11, 13, 14, 15, 17, 19, 20, 23, 25, 26, 29; Shutterstock: Bruno Ismael Silva Alves, (grunge texture) design element throughout, Bryan Solomon, (bottle) Cover, freesoulproduction, (leaves) Cover, Hein Nouwens, (hammer) Cover, Michele Paccione, (football) Cover, Miguel Angel Salinas Salinas, (tape) Cover, Nevena Radonja, (camera) Cover, Nikitina Karina, (string) Cover, PictureStudio, (tape measure) Cover, Slobodan Zivkovic, (leaves) Cover, vladis.studio, (glue, pen scissors) Cover

Printed and bound in China.

Contents

INTO THE WILD

There's nothing on TV. You've conquered all of your video games. You've looked all over the house and nothing looks fun. Now you're bored. What are you going to do?

It's time to get up and bust your boredom in the outdoors! You can build your own games, learn about nature and practise your sports skills. With a few things that you have around the house and with your imagination, there's no limit to what you can do outside.

Rain or shine – it doesn't matter what the weather is. There are great projects you can work on if you're alone or with friends. When you head outside, you can create your own entertainment. Just follow these simple directions and you'll be having too much fun outdoors to even think about boredom!

SAFETY FIRST

Some of these projects will require adult supervision, while others you'll be able to tackle on your own. Before you begin any project, make sure you have all the required tools and materials, and carefully read all the way through the instructions.

FEED THE BIRDS

MATERIALS

paper towels or newspaper

plastic knife

peanut butter

empty toilet roll tube

birdseed

paper plate

heavy-duty string (optional)

camera (optional)

bird identification book (optional)

Birds need to find a lot of food to survive, especially in winter. This easy-to-make bird feeder is fun, colourful and sure to bring countless birds outside your window. How many birds can you name?

1 Spread some paper towels or newspaper on an outdoor table.

2 With the plastic knife, spread peanut butter over the outside of the toilet roll tube. Be generous!

3 Pour some birdseed onto the paper plate, covering the surface.

4 Roll the tube over the birdseed. Apply some pressure to make sure that the tube is completely covered.

5 Run the string through the toilet roll tube and then tie the ends of the string to a tree branch. Or if you don't have any string, let the feeder sit right on a branch.

6 Step back and wait for the birds to come for a treat! Take pictures if you want or use a bird book to identify the different *species* of birds.

species group of plants or animals that share common characteristics

HERE, BIRDY

Different birds like different types of bird feed. Black oil sunflower seeds or shelled sunflower seeds are very popular with starlings, finches and nuthatches. Get a bird identification book from the public library or talk to a park ranger to learn more about the birds where you live.

TARGET TOSS

MATERIALS

large tarp with *grommets* at the corners

metre stick

marker pen

scissors

colourful duct tape

15 metres (50 feet) of nylon rope

a soccer ball, baseball, football or other type of ball

Wouldn't it be great if you had a back garden game that would also help you practise your sport skills? Now you do! This target toss game is easy to make, and it's fun to play alone. Target Toss is also easy to fold up and throw in the car to take along on camping trips and holidays. Want to raise the stakes? Invite some friends over and have a competition!

1 Spread the tarp on the ground or a flat surface.

2 Use the metre stick and marker pen to draw four to six different shapes spaced evenly on the tarp. These will become the target holes. They can be squares, triangles or circles. Make them different sizes so some are easier to hit than others. All of the holes should be large enough to fit the ball through.

grommet eyelet placed in a hole of a tarp or panel to protect a rope or cable passing through it, or to prevent the tarp or panel from being torn

3 Use the scissors to carefully cut out the shapes.

4 Use duct tape to frame the holes. Fold it over the edge of the hole so it creates a strong border.

5 Use the marker pen or duct tape to add point values to each hole. Smaller holes are harder to hit, so make them worth more points.

6 Cut the rope into four pieces. Tie a piece of the rope to each corner using the grommets. Hang the tarp from a tree or building.

TIP:
Make sure there is nothing behind the tarp that can be damaged by flying balls.

7 Grab a ball and start tossing! Get together with friends and have a competition. Who can score the most points in five throws?

15

10

PAVEMENT CHALK PAINT

MATERIALS

pavement chalk
(old broken pieces
will also work)

plastic bags

hammer

plastic containers
with lids

water

paintbrushes of
various sizes

Are you feeling artistic?
Pavement chalk is a fun way to
create colourful drawings on
the pavement or driveway. With
this simple project, you can turn
pavement chalk into paint. Time to
get your hands dirty and create your
next masterpiece!

1 Sort the pieces of pavement
chalk by colour. Put each colour
into its own plastic bag.

2 Using the hammer, carefully
pound the chalk through the
bag until it is powdery.

3 Empty each bag of powder into
its own plastic container.

4 Add 240 millilitres (1 cup) of
water to each container. Put the
lid on and shake the container
vigorously.

5 Take the new paint outside, grab
a paintbrush and start painting
on the pavement or driveway!

vigorous forceful

DISCOVER THE STARS

MATERIALS

- printable constellation cards
- paint or marker pens
- empty toilet roll or paper towel tube

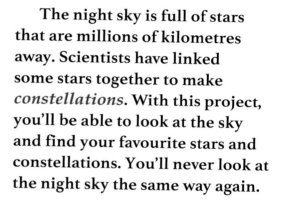

The night sky is full of stars that are millions of kilometres away. Scientists have linked some stars together to make *constellations*. With this project, you'll be able to look at the sky and find your favourite stars and constellations. You'll never look at the night sky the same way again.

1 With an adult's help, find a website with printable constellation cards. Or check out a book with maps of the constellations at the library. Study a few constellations, and find some favourites.

2 Using the paint or the markers, decorate the cardboard tube. This will be your pretend *telescope*. Longer tubes make better telescopes.

3 Using the constellation cards or book, choose a constellation to find in the sky.

constellation group of stars that forms a shape

telescope tool people use to look at objects in space; telescopes make objects in space look closer than they really are

TIP:

Cassiopeia is an easy constellation for starters. It looks like the letter W.

4 With an adult's supervision, go outside somewhere dark, such as a back garden or in the countryside. Close one eye and use the other to look through your new telescope. The telescope blocks unnecessary light and will help you focus on small parts of the sky, making it easier to see the constellations. How many constellations can you find?

PHOTO SAFARI

MATERIALS

a camera or mobile phone with photo capability

a safe place to explore

computer and printer

glue

small 10- by 15-cm (4- by 6-in) piece of cardboard

twigs or small branches

twine or string

Imagine you're an adventurer on a safari. All it takes is a camera and some ideas and you have an afternoon of outdoor fun. What will you choose for your safari topic? Wild animals? Creepy, crawly bugs? Challenge yourself and your friends with this photo safari! Meet up after the safari to compare your pictures.

TIP:
Try to pick a topic you enjoy and can find nearby.

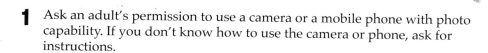

1 Ask an adult's permission to use a camera or a mobile phone with photo capability. If you don't know how to use the camera or phone, ask for instructions.

2 Choose a topic for your photo safari. You could try to find as many different kinds of birds, bugs or animals as you can. Perhaps you prefer road signs or different types of trees.

3 With an adult's supervision, find a safe place where you can roam around and discover a variety of your topic targets.

4 Start taking pictures! Experiment with different angles and camera settings to create fun and interesting photos. Lie on your back to get a different view. Try out the *panoramic* setting on your camera for a wide shot.

5 While you're taking pictures, keep an eye out for twigs that you could use to make your picture frame.

6 Get together and look at all of your photos! Have each person pick out his or her favourite photo.

panorama wide or complete view of an area

7 Ask an adult to help you print your favourite picture.

8 Glue your photo onto the piece of cardboard.

9 Use the twigs and twine to create a decorative frame around the edge of the photo. Simply glue the pieces in place however you'd like. Now it's time to admire your new work of nature art!

GIVE THIS A TRY:
Challenge yourself or friends to see who can find 10 different items first. Or create bingo cards and make it a game!

NEIGHBOURHOOD SCAVENGER HUNT

MATERIALS

pen and paper
a bucket or bag

When you're hunting for something to do, maybe it's a hunt that you need! A *scavenger hunt* is a game that gives you clues to find certain things. You'll have fun making a mad dash to find the things on your list. The list can be anything from random back garden items to different kinds of tree leaves. Compete with your friends to see who can finish first!

1 Create the scavenger hunt list. If you have multiple players, one person can be the judge and make the list. Or ask an adult to create one for you using items that can be found in the area where you will be playing.

2 The same person who made the list should also create clues to help you find the items. Clues are optional, but they make the game more fun and challenging.

3 Collect the items in a bag or bucket.

4 Be the first one to find all the items and win!

scavenger hunt game, typically played in an outdoor area, in which participants have to collect a number of random objects

TIP:

Try to think up a fun, themed list. How about things in your neighbourhood, such as a white letterbox, a rosebush and a garden ornament? Or head to the park and look for a park bench, a slide, a sandpit and a pine cone.

Scaveng
- ☐ Heart-shaped
- ☐ Flat rock
- ☑ Pine cone
- ☐ Dandelion
- ☐ Lizard
- ☐ Falls

GIANT LAWN GAME

MATERIALS

scissors

cardboard box

large roll of string

2 small stakes for string

4 cans of ground-marking spray paint in green, red, blue and yellow

paper and pencil

What's more fun than playing a board game? Playing a life-sized board game on your lawn! This simple version of Twister® can be created as big as you want so you can have any number of players.

TIP:
Do not use basic spray paint. This could kill the grass!

1 With an adult's help, cut a hole in the bottom of the cardboard box 15 centimetres (6 inches) in diameter.

2 Tie the string around one of the stakes. Push the stake into the ground. Stretch the string in the direction you would like to make your game board. Then tie the other end of the string to the other stake. Push the stake into the ground.

3 Using the string as a guide, make the first row of dots using one colour of spray paint. Use the box as a stencil to create circles.

4 Repeat step 3 with the other colours of spray paint to make the game board. There should be one row of each colour.

5 Wait a couple of hours for the spray paint to dry.

6 Cut eight small pieces of paper. Each piece of paper should be labelled for a body part or colour. For body parts, use: right hand, left hand, right foot and left foot. For colours, use the four colours of your spray paint.

7 Invite some friends over to play this classic game!

NEVER PLAYED?
HERE ARE THE RULES:

Three to five people should stand on the game board. A "caller" draws two paper slips: one body part and one colour. Then, he or she calls them out. For example, "Right hand, green!" Each player has to try to put his or her right hand on a green circle. Don't lose your balance!

RAINBOW BUBBLE SNAKES

MATERIALS

washing up liquid

bowl

water

golden syrup (optional)

knife or scissors

plastic bottle

cotton flannel or sock

elastic band

food colouring in multiple colours

Rainbow bubble snakes look like long, brightly coloured serpents! They're easy to make, and your friends won't believe the amazing bubble snakes you can create.

TIP:

A little bit of the golden syrup can make your bubbles stronger, but it is not necessary. Add a tablespoon of syrup during step 1 if using.

1 Add 45 millilitres (3 tablespoons) of washing up liquid to a bowl. Then add 240 millilitres (1 cup) of water to the bowl. Stir the *solution* together. Let the bowl sit for a few hours.

2 With an adult's help, cut the bottom off the plastic bottle.

3 Place the flannel or sock on the bottom of the bottle, completely covering the opening. Secure the flannel or sock to the bottle with the elastic band.

4 Place a few drops of food colouring on the fabric. Use several colours to cover the surface of the flannel or sock.

5 Dip the fabric end of the bottle into the bubble solution. Make sure the fabric gets completely soaked.

6 Blow through the drinking end of the bottle, and watch your rainbow bubble snakes appear! Who can create the longest snake?

solution mixture made of a substance that has been dissolved in another substance

GLOSSARY

constellation group of stars that forms a shape

grommet eyelet placed in a hole of a tarp or panel to protect a rope or cable passing through it, or to prevent the tarp or panel from being torn

panorama wide or complete view of an area

scavenger hunt game, typically played in an outdoor area, in which participants have to collect a number of random objects

solution mixture made of a substance that has been dissolved in another substance

species group of plants or animals that share common characteristics

telescope tool people use to look at objects in space; telescopes make objects in space look closer than they really are

vigorous forceful

READ MORE

Let's Go Outside: Imaginative Outdoor Games and Projects for Kids, Steph Scott and Katie Akers (Batsford, 2015)

Maker Projects for Kids Who Love Exploring the Outdoors (Be a Maker!), Sarah Levete (Crabtree, 2016)

Outdoor Science Lab for Kids: 52 Family-Friendly Experiments for the Yard, Garden, Playground, and Park (Lab Series), Liz Lee Heinecke (Quarry Books, 2016)

WEBSITES

www.persil.co.uk/activities-for-kids/
Explore arts, crafts, games and recipes that can be done indoors or outdoors.

www.wildlifetrusts.org/discovery
Explore, play in and learn about nature with The Wildlife Trusts.

INDEX